Original title:
Life's Like a Good Joke—It Doesn't Always Make Sense

Copyright © 2025 Creative Arts Management OÜ
All rights reserved.

Author: Gabriel Kingsley
ISBN HARDBACK: 978-1-80566-108-5
ISBN PAPERBACK: 978-1-80566-403-1

Tales of the Unexpected

A cat wore a hat, what a sight,
While dogs danced merrily through the night.
The moon cracked a grin, stars giggled loud,
As socks found their mates in a fluffy cloud.

A fish learned to fly, so bold and free,
While cows strummed guitars under the tree.
Chickens in suits played cards with the sun,
Every mishap was just another fun run.

The Hilarity of Misunderstanding

A baker mistook dough for a pet,
And trained it to dance with no threat.
The loaf waltzed and spun on the floor,
While flour fell down like never before.

A frog thought it was a prince in a play,
He jumped into ponds, come what may.
But no kiss awaited, just ripples so wide,
As laughter erupted from folks on the side.

Ballet of the Bewildered

The trees held a gala, all dressed in green,
With ribbons and twirls, they put on a scene.
And squirrels in tutus performed with delight,
As acorns cheered from their seats, what a sight!

A dog in a bow tie thought he could sing,
As bees lent their buzz, adding to the fling.
The wind played the flute, a jolly old tune,
And the stars in the sky danced beneath the moon.

Whimsical Whirls of Reality

A turtle raced by on a skateboard fast,
While time sighed and laughed, wishing it passed.
Clouds spun like tops on an unseen string,
As giggles erupted from everything.

An octopus juggled, what skill he displayed,
With ink blots that colored the glade.
And shadows of laughter lit up the ground,
In a world where confusion and joy abound.

Wit's Brightest Disguises

In the circus of thoughts, clowns do prance,
With mismatched shoes and a silly dance.
Juggled emotions, they soar and fall,
Each twist and turn, a chuckle for all.

Tickle the fancy, don't take a stand,
With pies in the face and a rubber band.
Laughter erupts like a fizzy drink,
Absurdities swirl, make you stop and think.

Far from the norm, the oddballs bloom,
In topsy-turvy rooms that spell out doom.
But laughter shines bright through the jumbled frame,
For wit's wild jest is the heart of the game.

So grab a balloon, let the giggles spill,
Embrace the madness, feel the thrill.
In the punchline's punch, a thread to unwind,
From chaos and giggles, wisdom you'll find.

Pawprints of the Playful Universe

Stars twinkle down, like mischief in space,
Whiskers of laughter adorn every face.
The universe giggles, it tumbles and spins,
Chasing its tail where the storyline begins.

Each moment's a riddle that tickles the mind,
With cat-like leaps, we wander and bind.
Ticklish shadows dance on the wall,
As we ponder the meaning, we just trip and fall.

From puddles of rain to the clouds in the sky,
The punchlines fall flat, oh me, oh my!
Yet every stumble leads to a cheer,
In the festival of folly, we conquer our fear.

So step in the puddles, splash with delight,
Let whimsy take over, into the night.
With pawprints left behind, we find in our chase,
That humor's the thread that binds our embrace.

Unpredictable Twists of Fate

A banana peel slips, oh what a fall,
In the circus of dreams, we all stand tall.
Laughter erupts as plans go astray,
Dancing through chaos, we smile anyway.

Jokes in the wind, tickle our ears,
Twists of fortune, shedding our fears.
Witty remarks, like confetti in air,
Spin us around; we haven't a care.

The Lighthearted Labyrinth

Through mazes of whimsy, we wander and roam,
Searching for logic, but finding our home.
A riddle of moments, unraveling fast,
We giggle at puzzles, they're meant to last.

In this jolly maze, confusion's the key,
With chuckles that echo, we're wild and free.
Dodging the cause of our ticklish delight,
Fumbling and tumbling, all through the night.

Silly Threads of Destiny

Spinning our fate like a yarn on a reel,
Knots of hilarity, oh, what a deal!
Wit weaves the fabric, stitching up glee,
As we trip on the threads, we giggle with glee.

Each twist is a tale that's seldom profound,
Where logic's a jester, just spinning around.
We wear mismatched socks and a grin on our face,
Embracing the silliness, we find our place.

The Absurd Art of Living

With crayons we sketch what we dream to be true,
In a world of mayhem, we doodle and spew.
The canvas of chaos welcomes our strokes,
Let's paint our own punchlines, tickling folks.

Every mishap and blunder turns shiny and bright,
Laughter's the beacon that glimmers at night.
As we juggle the nonsense, we find our sweet grace,
In the comedy show of this wild, wild place.

Whimsical Whispers of Fate

Woke up to the sun's bright glare,
A sock on the cat's back, in the air.
Birds tweet in silly, off-key tones,
While my coffee is just a cup of stones.

Dancing with shadows on the floor,
The toaster pops out a slice of lore.
Chased by thoughts both wild and free,
Like a fish that dreams of being a tree.

The Riddle of Silly Days

Why do pancakes prefer the sky?
Because syrup loves to fly high!
Juggling oranges in a top hat,
A duck in boots, what's up with that?

Whispers of giggles in the breeze,
A tree that sneezes, oh what a tease!
Holding hands with the bubbling brook,
Where time plays tricks, just take a look.

Giggles in the Grand Design

A clock that dances, ticking out of tune,
While rabbits plan a trip to the moon.
Clouds wear hats made of candy floss,
Stumbling on paths made of gloss.

Singing shoes with untied laces,
Find laughter in the silliest places.
Every step turns into a jest,
In this merry game, we are all guests.

Absurdity's Dance

Riding a bicycle made of cheese,
While gentlemen frogs bow with ease.
A sandwich talks, and what does it say?
"Please don't eat, I'm here to play!"

Under a moon that's a plate of pie,
Twinkling stars wink, oh my, oh my!
In the garden where laughter blooms,
Absurdity's dance fills all the rooms.

Mosaic of the Peculiar

In a world where ducks may fly,
And cats run businesses by and by,
The sun might dance, the moon might sing,
A jigsaw puzzle with no clear king.

With laughter bursting in the street,
A neighbor's llama's on repeat,
We wear our quirks like a badge of pride,
As round the merry goofballs glide.

A banana phone rings out of tune,
While squirrels gather 'neath a laughing moon,
Each moment filled with odd delight,
Turn up the silly, forget the fright.

So gather 'round for stories spun,
Of mishaps caught in webs of fun,
For every twist and turn we make,
There's joy found in the gag and quake.

Jests Carved in Time

Tick-tock, the clocks go slow,
As socks lose mates in the laundry flow,
A tumble here, a stumble there,
Surprises hiding everywhere.

With every step, you just might trip,
Over a thought or a coffee sip,
Dance like no one's watching you,
With moves so silly they break right through.

A cat with glasses reads a book,
While pigeons gossip on the nook,
In corners where shadows play and tease,
Are secrets shared by buzzing bees.

So chalk it up to whims of fate,
Embrace the jest, don't hesitate,
For every laugh that fills the air,
Is a smile sent from somewhere rare.

The Joy in Misfit Moments

A fish on land wearing a hat,
Chewing gum with a clever cat,
Confusion reigns in every peak,
As giggles slip through whispers sleek.

The toast may burn, the soup might spill,
Yet in the chaos, there's a thrill,
For every bump and every bruise,
A new adventure we can choose.

Umbrellas upside down at noon,
With rainbows dancing to a tune,
What oddities the day can bring,
A tapestry where we all sing.

So grab a pie and toss it high,
Let flying desserts be the reason why,
In moments bizarre, the heart takes flight,
Laughter is born from the oddest sight.

Quips that Connect Us

Two mismatched socks on a sunny day,
Wander together, come what may,
A bird on the ground tries to play chess,
In a world that thrives on sheer silliness.

When buttons lose their charming threads,
They invent stories behind our heads,
And every crack in the sidewalk told,
Is a memory cherished, a joy to hold.

A laughter shared across the room,
With echoes that chase away the gloom,
In quirky tales that somehow unite,
We bask in the glow of pure delight.

So let's spin yarns of laughter bright,
In a carnival of thought and light,
For through the twist in everyone's tale,
We find the laughter that will prevail.

Sunshine in the Absurd.

In a world where cats can fly,
And penguins wear a tie,
The sun winks with a grin,
As rainbows dance and spin.

A frog in boots sings loud,
Making laughter from the crowd,
When the clock strikes a tune,
We'll all dance 'neath the moon.

A giraffe sips coffee straight,
While the squirrels plan their fate,
Juggling nuts in a tree,
Oh, what a sight to see!

When life delivers a pie,
Right in the face, oh my!
We wipe cream from our eyes,
And burst into joyful sighs.

Laughter in the Shadows

In the dark where shadows play,
A ticklish ghost will sway,
With every spooky howl,
Comes a chuckle, a joyful growl.

A raccoon in a hat, you see,
Is plotting its next spree,
Underneath the starry sky,
Where the night is full of pie.

The moon cracks a little joke,
While the stars begin to poke,
At a kitten chasing light,
Mischief wraps the night tight.

Within the giggles of the breeze,
Lurks humor amid the trees,
For when the shadows creep near,
Laughter is always here.

The Punchline of Existence

With a flip and a tumble, we start,
Every day a quirky art,
Where banana peels await,
To make us laugh, don't hesitate.

A fish wears boots, how absurd!
It flops and rolls, so unheard,
In puddles of mirth, we dive,
Hoping this whimsy will thrive.

The toaster sings a sweet tune,
While socks have a dance in June,
Every hiccup, a brand-new twist,
In this gag we can't resist.

As we juggle lemons and dreams,
Reality bursts at the seams,
In the punchline, we all blend,
Where laughter will never end.

When Chaos Wears a Smile

Amidst the chaos, laughter rings,
A circus of curious things,
Where teacups spin in delight,
And elephants take flight.

The jellybeans begin to prance,
In a whimsical, sweet dance,
Lollipops wobble in cheer,
As giggles are drawing near.

A jester juggles the absurd,
With antics that stir the bird,
Pies in hand, the jesters beam,
Together we'll all dream.

With a wink and a twirl so fine,
Chaos takes its place in line,
For in laughter, we find the key,
To unlock our wildest spree.

The Jigsaw of Joy and Confusion

Pieces scatter everywhere,
Finding the shape of delight.
Some fit but never stay,
Colors clash in morning light.

Laughter hides in the chaos,
A puzzle with missing parts.
Flat jokes stumble in the dark,
Yet bloom like gentle arts.

Serious faces crack wide,
When antics take center stage.
Jigsaws of giggles collide,
In the heart of every age.

So let's dance with a wink,
As we search for the next clue.
In this maze of funny thoughts,
There's always more to pursue.

Tickled by Uncertainty

Wobbly paths lie ahead,
Each twist a chuckle anew.
Hang onto silly moments,
They stretch our view.

Faces grin in confusion,
As plans spin like a top.
Laughter's contagious rhythm,
Makes troubles drop.

Question marks float like balloons,
In the breeze of a sunny day.
Nonsense cloaked in sunshine,
Guides our playful sway.

Swinging on swings of odd chance,
We find joy in the ride.
Embrace the muddled mystery,
With humor as our guide.

Laughter Echoes in Unexpected Places

Whispers of giggles in the hall,
Where shadows twirl and tease.
A good pun leaps from a wall,
　Turning worries into ease.

Ticklish moments greet the night,
　As stars blink in surprise.
Laughter's feather takes its flight,
　Painting dreams in the skies.

In the corners of lost thoughts,
　Smiles ripple through the blur.
We stumble on joy's bright spots,
　In this quirky whirl.

Hungry for more of the wild,
We'll chase what's hard to find.
In every corner, a giggling child,
　Reminds us to unwind.

Quirky Threads of Existence

Threads tangle in odd designs,
Weaving tales of the absurd.
Random moments intertwine,
Creating laughs unheard.

Life veers left, then spins right,
Dance steps chaotically bold.
Through the mix, we embrace light,
With stories to be told.

A joke nestled in surprise,
Sprouts laughter in our path.
Every twist, a playful rise,
Scoffing at the past's math.

Through the quilt of quirky quests,
We chase the colors that shine.
In this tapestry, we find rest,
Where silly hearts align.

Laughter Laced with Uncertainty

In a world of slips and trips,
Where giggles spring from awkward pips,
The punchlines dance, then take a dive,
As we all wonder, 'Will this thrive?'

With every twist, a smile creeps,
Through puzzled thoughts, the humor leaps.
When plans go sideways, don't you fret,
Embrace the silly, it's a bet!

A jester's grin in every plight,
As silly dreams take flight each night.
The laughter comes from messy scenes,
In life's grand play, we're all routines.

So hold your sides and don't despair,
For laughter blooms from thin-air flair.
In chaos wrapped, there's joy to find,
A chuckle shared, and hearts unbind.

The Unexpected Essence of Humor

When irony walks hand in hand,
With playful pranks and plans unplanned,
We find the joy in blunders sweet,
As quick wit dances on our feet.

Each twist and turn, a tale unspools,
We play the part of loving fools.
With every slip, the laughter swells,
A symphony of chuckle spells.

Beneath the frowns and tangled threads,
The humor's found in frayed edges.
A wink exchanged in uncertain times,
The world erupts in absurd rhymes.

In jest, we find our way to cope,
A rolling laugh, the sweetest hope.
For while we stumble through the fray,
Laughter shines to light the way.

Chuckling with the Cosmos

Stars twinkle high, mischief in sight,
As comets whiz with giggles bright.
The universe plays its cosmic chess,
In moments wild, we just confess.

A galaxy spills its secrets wide,
In cosmic jests, there's nowhere to hide.
We're stardust wrapped in smiles and sighs,
Unraveling wonders in winking skies.

Each black hole has a laugh or two,
As planets spin in playful hue.
A universe where nonsense thrives,
In the chaos, our spirit jives.

So when the cosmos cracks a grin,
Join in the dance—it's where we win.
For joy lingers in the vast unknown,
With laughter echoing, we find our home.

Shadows that Smirk Back

In twilight's grip, the shadows play,
With mischief lurking, night meets day.
They twirl about in silly glee,
As if to mock reality.

Each corner turned, a twist of fate,
Surprising us with fun debates.
When laughter rings, the fears all fade,
With every chuckle, doubts evade.

Reflected glances tell a tale,
Of how humor must prevail.
In jests, we find the tricks of light,
Where shadows smirk, our spirits ignite.

So gather 'round, let laughter soar,
In the shadows, there's always more.
For when we face the dark with grace,
The smirking shadows become our space.

Mirthful Mysteries Unveiled

A cat wears shoes, how absurd,
Chasing shadows and the chirping bird.
Laughter dances in curious air,
With each twist, it's hard to compare.

Bananas might wear a bright blue hat,
While turtles strut like they own the mat.
Winking puppets on a threadbare stage,
Delivering giggles as they act their age.

A knock at the door, what a surprise,
It's a pie that's begun to rise!
Butterflies giggle in the morning sun,
As riddles unfold and jokes come undone.

In the heart of chaos, joy does bloom,
Finding treasure in a cluttered room.
Every chuckle, a spark of delight,
Embracing the silly with all of our might.

Lopsided Lessons

A fish in a hat looks very grand,
Yet can't quite swim in the dry land.
Juggling lemons with a grin so wide,
In this circus, there's nowhere to hide.

A giraffe rides a bike, quite a scene,
Twirling and whirling, like in a dream.
What's wrong with this picture, they ask in jest,
But laughter erupts, and we're feeling blessed.

Cracking eggs while dancing on a floor,
Yolk spills out, now isn't that lore?
Stumbling in rhythm, we trip and we sway,
But each silly moment is here to stay.

Hearts ache with joy, wrapped in a joke,
Finding the punchline when we're all awoke.
So toss up your hat and laugh out loud,
In this wobbly world, let humor be proud.

The Quirk of Being

A dog wearing glasses, going to class,
While singing a tune with plenty of sass.
Socks on a rooster, strutting about,
You can't help but chuckle; it's what life's about.

Pancakes flip like they've got a past,
Each syrupy layer, a question asked.
A fish with a tale, spinning around,
With giggles erupted at every sound.

A robot that dances with clumsy flair,
Cups of warm coffee fly through the air.
What's left unspoken floats here on the breeze,
Causing rumbles of laughter that aim to please.

In this wacky world, let's make it bright,
With whimsical charm that invites delight.
Every twist and turn, a playful embrace,
In the silliness found, we all find our place.

Sarcasm in the Silence

Whispers of trouble hang in the air,
A sock puppet's gaze is quite the affair.
Nod of a cabbage, smug on a throne,
With not much to say, yet clearly not alone.

A wink from the moon, so full of spite,
Queries linger in the dark of the night.
With sarcasm wrapped in a riddle's crest,
The silence will giggle, let humor manifest.

Frogs in a lounge wear tuxedos and ties,
Sipping on nectar with exaggerated sighs.
Every chuckle's a secret, a well-kept delight,
In the space of quiet, they find the spotlight.

So tip your hat to what's been unspooled,
In odd little moments, we've all been schooled.
With laughter and whispers floating on air,
It's the absurdity found that we all can share.

Gags Suspended in Time

In a town where clocks don't tick,
Laughter echoes, it plays a trick.
The pigeons wear hats, quite absurd,
And the whispers of trees go unheard.

A cat rides a bike with great flair,
While the sun dances wildly in air.
Bananas do somersaults in glee,
As kids fly kites made of seaweed free.

The moon throws pies at passing skates,
While dogs discuss their lunch dates.
And the stars sometimes play hide and seek,
In a world that wobbles, no need to speak.

So grab a seat, stay for the show,
With this circus, your heart will glow.
Each twist and turn a surprise in disguise,
Gags suspended, for all to rise.

Nuances of Nonsense

On Mondays, the cows wear shoes,
While goldfish recite the daily news.
The chair squeaks jokes to the worn-out floor,
As the ceiling fan grins, wanting more.

A sandwich debates with a cup of tea,
On who's the real star of the spree.
Outside, the wind sings a silly tune,
And the grass tickles toes like a cartoon.

Rainbows slide down the slippery street,
As umbrellas break out in a dance so sweet.
The clouds shape-shift into a game of charades,
In a realm where logic merely fades.

So join in this whimsical parade,
Where nonsense and joy are carefully laid.
In nuances found, laughter will cling,
And the heart will soar on nonsense wings.

Witty Wonders in the Ordinary

Teacups chatter on a rainy day,
While butterflies paint the skies gray.
The doorknob tells secrets to shoes,
And the walls crack up with silly views.

Garden gnomes are practicing mime,
As the trees decide it's perfect time.
A spoon tells a fork it's quite a flex,
In kitchen tales that make no sense.

Mailboxes open their mouths so wide,
To share the tales of the things inside.
And windows wink at passersby,
In this odd world where giggles fly.

So find the wonders in what you see,
The quirks of life, a joyous spree.
With every twist that catches your eye,
The ordinary spins a laugh, oh my!

The Punchline of What's Real

In a cafe where the chairs gossip,
Sugar cubes perform a wobbly flip.
The clocks tick backwards just for fun,
While croissants giggle under the sun.

A tree wears glasses to read a book,
And the tablecloth gives a sideways look.
The coffee splashes jokes in the cup,
While pastries loll about, livin' it up.

Strange clouds shout rhymes in puffs of air,
As the sidewalk cartwheels without a care.
In a place where logic takes a break,
The punchline waits for the big mistake.

So roll with the quirks that come your way,
Embrace the oddities, let them sway.
For in this realm, laughter reveals,
The best punchlines are what life conceals.

The Punchline of Tomorrow

A twist of fate, a scribbled note,
We laugh and sigh, it's all remote.
The punchline waits in shadows cast,
While moments flash, but seldom last.

With every slip, we find our way,
A stumble here, a game to play.
Tomorrow's joke, a glint of light,
As chuckles chase the fading night.

We juggle dreams, both high and low,
A giggle hides in sorrow's glow.
Each quip and quirk, a tale retold,
In jest, we find our hearts unfold.

So raise a glass to clumsy fate,
Where funny moments never wait.
For in this dance of sense and sound,
The laughter blooms when hope is found.

Curated Chaos

In tangled webs where jokes align,
We chase the punchlines, sip the wine.
Awkward pauses, awkward smiles,
Life's wild ride, it spans the miles.

A silent scream, a muffled cheer,
The irony feels oh so near.
With every twist and turn we take,
We're caught in laughter's grand mistake.

The clock ticks slow, the punchlines fly,
Around the bends, we laugh and cry.
In chaos brewed with comic flair,
We find our joy in just a stare.

So hug the absurd, embrace the storm,
In curated chaos, moods transform.
For laughter rings when plans collide,
In silly fumbles, jokes reside.

Raucous Revelations

Beneath the surface, secrets hum,
As laughter sprinkles, chaos comes.
Raucous whispers fill the air,
With every jest, we learn to dare.

Revelations dance on silly tongues,
As folly sings, our hearts are young.
In every stumble, truth revealed,
Through humor's lens, our fate is sealed.

The mystery lies in wrong turns made,
In comic trials, we're never swayed.
With every grin, the wisdom flows,
A jest to lighten heavy woes.

So raise a toast to messy grace,
To joyful hearts that run the race.
For every laugh that breaks the frame,
We find our way back home again.

The Humor Hidden in Heartbreak

When tears are shed, a giggle sneaks,
Amidst the pain, the humor peaks.
In shattered dreams, a chuckle lies,
Where sorrow wears a funny guise.

A cartoon heart, with patches sewn,
In awkward tales, we're never alone.
Through flippant jests, we bear our scars,
As laughter twirls beneath the stars.

Each tear we shed, a joke misplaced,
Yet finding joy through love's embrace.
The paradox of smiles and cries,
In hurt, we learn, in joy, we rise.

So hold on tight, embrace the ride,
In heartbreak's grip, let laughter guide.
For hidden gems in pain will show,
The humor's there, just let it flow.

When Sense Takes a Holiday

In the morning, socks don't match,
Dancing shoes on the way to catch.
Coffee spills, the cat looks amused,
As the calendar shows a day to snooze.

Birds sing tunes that twist and swirl,
A dog in a hat gives a boy a whirl.
With a hiccup, the tea kettle flies,
And laughter erupts from all surprised.

A banana slips on its own peel,
Who knew the floor had such appeal?
Jokes in the air, like bubbles rise,
A world where whimsy brightly sighs.

When order leaves, and chaos thrives,
The joy in folly truly arrives.
Whispering echoes of silly delight,
As nonsense dances into the night.

Jesters of the Everyday

In the market, a fishy sale,
A man in a tutu, without a trail.
Chickens cluck out a might tune,
While pickles waltz beneath the moon.

A cat on a skateboard takes a spin,
And a dog with glasses grins and grins.
With every grocery bag that spills,
Laughter bubbles, and joy fulfills.

The sun wears shades, playing it cool,
While wise old owls pretend to drool.
Amidst the mundane, silliness creeps,
Tickling our hearts, it never sleeps.

From every corner, giggles escape,
Life's a circus, with no real shape.
Jesters abound, in roles so bizarre,
We smile and chuckle, wherever we are.

Curly Queues of Curiosity

Balloons float up to touch the sun,
While the dogs and the ducks decide to run.
A little boy trips over a kite,
But laughter erupts; it feels so right.

Marbles roll in a zigzag dance,
As ants in a line seem to prance.
Sidewalk chalk draws tales so wild,
Every mistake, a charm unbilled.

Questions swirl like leaves in the breeze,
Why do we chase, why do we freeze?
Inquirers laugh, seeking the odd,
Finding fairies in the backyard sod.

With every twist, the world appears,
Encouraging smiles, dismissing fears.
Curly queues of thoughts, surreal and merry,
They tickle our minds, light as a fairy.

The Irony in Ordinary

A man in a suit rides a bike,
A child in a tie decides to hike.
Coffee stains on a blank report,
Mistakes make for the best retort.

The cat sleeps soundly on a mat,
While socks form a pile next to the spat.
Dishes clink and echo delight,
As dinner's a game of chance tonight.

Each sigh is a giggle, each frown a grin,
In the pages of life, we dive right in.
Ordinary days, though mundane they seem,
Are a canvas where laughter beams.

With irony wrapped in a lovely bow,
We take our turns, we ebb and flow.
Through highs and lows, with humor we cope,
Finding joy in each twist of hope.

Laughter in Shadows

In the corner, shadows dance,
Flickering light, a silly chance.
Jokes hang heavy in the air,
Tickling ribs, a playful dare.

The cat wears glasses, quite a sight,
Trying to read with all its might.
The fridge hums a quirky tune,
While spoons argue with the moon.

A fish in shoes, swimming free,
Chatters about its bent decree.
With every giggle, room grows bright,
In the shadows, laughter takes flight.

Embrace the chuckles, cheeky glee,
In the weirdness, we find the key.
For when you least expect the jest,
The heart feels light, the soul feels blessed.

The Absurdity of Clarity

A clock that laughs while it ticks,
Its hands are playing silly tricks.
Time's a jester in disguise,
With punchlines hidden in the skies.

The sun wears sunglasses, oh so cool,
While shadows gather for a duel.
Clouds debate the color blue,
And rainbows sprout like flowers do.

Nonsense rules the daily grind,
Wisdom found in what's unkind.
Yet in this chaos, joys ignite,
Finding clarity in the blight.

So let the weirdness be your guide,
In silly realms where truths abide.
For every riddle has its glee,
Unraveling the absurdity.

Punchlines and Paradoxes

A penguin waddles into a bar,
Orders ice cream, that's bizarre!
The bartender blinks in sheer surprise,
As laughter bubbles, brightens eyes.

A horse wearing shoes tries to dance,
With clumsy steps, a goofy prance.
Every misstep breeds a cheer,
In paradoxes, joy is near.

A cat who sings an opera tune,
Competes with frogs beneath the moon.
Every croak a clever quip,
Laughter flows like a comic trip.

So when the world feels strange and weird,
Remember all the fun we've cheered.
Each punchline's just a twist of fate,
Revealing joy we celebrate.

Whims of the Unseen

Invisible sprites hold a debate,
Over the quirks that make us late.
The chairs conspire behind closed doors,
As laughter echoes, never bores.

A sandwich talks on the kitchen shelf,
Wonders if it's still itself.
The toaster giggles with delight,
As butter flies in joyful flight.

Strange omens in a friendly crowd,
Chicken in a suit feels so proud.
With every glance, the smiles grow,
In unseen worlds, the laughter flows.

So dance with whims that tickle the air,
Finding the joy in the silly affair.
For in the unseen, we find our song,
And celebrate where we belong.

Nonsense Wrapped in Wisdom

In the kingdom of jest, where giggles reign,
The cat wears a hat, it's all so insane.
Pies fly in the air with a whimpering tune,
While wise old frogs discuss the light of the moon.

Riddles wrapped in candy, sweet flavors of doubt,
A squirrel plays chess, while the birds all shout.
Laughter dances lightly upon the grass green,
In this foolish realm, the quirkiest is seen.

The clocks melt like butter, draped on the wall,
And whispers of wisdom in laughter stand tall.
Embrace the absurd, for the punchline is near,
In jest, there's a truth we all hold dear.

So tip your hats low, to the jesters we meet,
With smiles that twinkle and antics so sweet.
Let nonsense remind us, in mirth we may find,
The wisdom that dances, unwrapped, unconfined.

Surreal Smiles at Sunrise

When the sun greets the day with a silly grin,
And shadows do tango, how can we begin?
With toast in a tutu, it dances around,
While laughter awakens without making a sound.

The coffee spills secrets, as cream swirls in glee,
A dog serenades all the ducks by the tree.
Each moment's absurd, yet there's beauty, it's true,
In the whirl of the whimsical, we start anew.

Giggles at breakfast, where pancakes play tricks,
And syrup like laughter, flows thick with quick flicks.
A sunbeam peeks in, with a wink and a nod,
In the dawn's cheerful chaos, we feel quite awed.

So step into the morning, with quirks in your heart,
Embrace all the nonsense, be ready to start.
For surreal smiles parade in the glow of the rays,
Brightening our souls in the comical haze.

Chuckles in the Confusion

Amidst the mad chatter where goats wear bow ties,
Confusion does reign, yet it's brightened by skies.
A bicycle rolls past, with a fish in the seat,
And upside-down umbrellas march down the street.

The clouds play charades, in a game quite absurd,
While trees share their secrets without a word.
Pigeons wear glasses; they lecture with pride,
As giggles erupt from the river's wild side.

Why do the rabbits wear socks on their feet?
And why does the moon dip to the tune of a beat?
In the riddle of chaos, with chuckles a-flare,
We find the sweet nonsense that hangs in the air.

So let's raise a toast, to the tipsy and fun,
To the quirks that unite us, while laughter's begun.
In the maze of confusion, we dance and we sway,
For humor's the thread that brightens our day.

The Playful Pen of Fate

With ink made of giggles, and paper of dreams,
Destiny scribbles in surreal little streams.
A turtle in sneakers races down the lane,
Writing tales of whimsy in the drizzle and rain.

In the tapestry woven, with stitches of cheer,
The pencil's a wand, and the sketches are clear.
Monkeys wear spectacles and read from old books,
While flowers burst into laughter with whimsical looks.

Every turn in the plot is a chuckle bestowed,
With twists that are silly, and paths that explode.
Why chase after plans that are neat and well laid?
When the joy of the moment begins with a shade?

So let's tip our hats, to the quirk of our fate,
For life's meant for giggles, not themes that are straight.
The playful pen writes in colors so bright,
With laughter as ink, we'll scribe our delight.

Baffling Truths in Wit

In laughter's maze, we stumble round,
Twists and turns in jest are found.
A punchline lands, yet leaves us lost,
In a giggle's grip, we pay the cost.

The world spins jokes that defy logic,
Like a cat who thinks it's hypnotic.
We scratch our heads at comic flair,
Wondering why we giggle, stare.

A rubber chicken on a throne,
Wearing glasses, all alone.
Its beak speaks wisdom, odd yet bright,
In quirky tales of day and night.

So laugh with me at baffled truths,
In a tumble of jokes like old sleuths.
Embrace the quirky, the strange, the wild,
Be cheerful like a curious child.

The Humor Hidden in Silence

In quiet moments, chuckles bloom,
An awkward grin fills up the room.
When words escape, we find the fun,
In silent games, it's never done.

A wink, a nod, a sly embrace,
In mute exchanges, we find our place.
The simplest glances spark delight,
In silence, laughter takes to flight.

A tickled tummy, an unspoken nudge,
In stillness, joy can't help but budge.
No need for chatter, no grand reveal,
Just shared smiles, a playful deal.

So in the hush, let giggles rise,
With every twinkle in our eyes.
Finding humor where few dare roam,
In laughter's grasp, we feel at home.

Follies of the Heart

To love is sometimes quite absurd,
Like a clumsy dance, without a word.
With every stumble, a comedy play,
Two hearts collide in a charming way.

A heart in knots, a silly affair,
We wear our feelings just like a flare.
With giggling birds and hearts that race,
In follies of love, we find our place.

Mixed signals send us into a spin,
Yet in such chaos, we'll always win.
For every fumble brings us near,
A shared laugh, that's why we're here.

Through quirks and blunders, we'll stay true,
With laughter's spark lighting up the view.
So raise a toast to love so bold,
In follies of heart, true joy unfolds.

Smiles Between the Lines

In every story that we share,
Beneath the surface, humor's there.
A twist of fate, a laugh-out-loud,
In written words, we feel so proud.

Between the lines, the punchlines hide,
In clever quips, we take the ride.
With every chapter, laughter creeps,
In meme-like wisdom, joy leaps.

A plot so rich, yet light as air,
On pages filled with love and care.
We scribble jokes in margins wide,
A secret world, our hearts abide.

So read aloud and share the fun,
In cozy moments, our laughter's spun.
For smiles are inked on every page,
In tales of life, we break the cage.

The Irony of Everyday Heroes

In capes of dust, they stride along,
With mismatched socks, they hum a song.
A spatula wields the sword of fate,
As chaos reigns, they still feel great.

The grocery list, a battle plan,
With carts as steeds, they take a stand.
Against the shelves stacked high with snack,
Their hearts are bold, but skills they lack.

With spilled milk floods, a laugh erupts,
They juggle woes, like circus pups.
The ironies spun, so wide and free,
In this grand farce, who's the hero, we see?

So raise a glass to those in plight,
In everyday suits, they fight the fight.
A wink and smile, the world feels bright,
For every joker brings delight.

Finding Wisdom in Play

In fields of laughter, the children roam,
Searching for treasures, far from home.
A pebble's wisdom, a leaf's delight,
As giggles dance in the fading light.

In games of tag, the truth unfurls,
Where merry mayhem conquers worlds.
The king of silly, crowned with grace,
In playful banter, we find our place.

With tumble and roll, the lessons blend,
In folly's arms, we learn and mend.
For jesters whisper in the breeze,
That wisdom hides where we feel at ease.

So let us play, abandon the wise,
In silly moments, happiness lies.
We stumble upon pure, blissful sway,
In the clown's embrace, we find our way.

Jesters in the Hall of Time

In corridors echoing with laughter's chime,
The jesters dance, defying time.
With painted smiles and playful jibes,
They spin the tales of our wild tribes.

Through ticking clocks and pastel dreams,
Their playful antics burst at the seams.
Whispers of wisdom, like sliding doors,
Unfold in giggles, in cosmic scores.

Each folly scribed in stardust's glow,
They teach us how to bend and flow.
For irony sparkles in every jest,
As laughter's warmth puts worries to rest.

In this fine hall, they reign supreme,
Weaving truth within each gleam.
So join the dance, let humor shine,
For jesters craft the grand design.

Revelations Wrapped in Punchlines

Beneath the surface of every jest,
Lies a revelation, a tiny quest.
For every laugh, there's a hidden truth,
Wrapped in humor, unearthing youth.

In jokes we find the sides of life,
The happy moments and the strife.
Each punchline a key, unlocking the door,
To wisdom waiting, forevermore.

With giggles echoing through the air,
We discover comfort in laughter's care.
For every whimsy, a story unfolds,
In the realms of jokes, the heart beholds.

So gather 'round, share a silly tale,
Where laughter's ship will always sail.
With every chuckle, the world aligns,
In the revelry wrapped within punchlines.

Serendipity's Comic Relief

A banana peels right on cue,
Slips me into laughter, so true.
The cat wears a hat, oh what a sight,
Dancing on walls, under moonlight.

Trips and stumbles, each twist unfolds,
Laughter, a treasure, more precious than gold.
Life a stage where the clowns bloom,
Painting our worries with a cosmic broom.

The sun sneezed, clouds took a bow,
While I sip coffee, a cow says 'Wow!'
Wit spins tales that dance through the air,
In this strange circus, nothing's unfair.

So join the march of the silly parade,
Where quirks and giggles are never delayed.
With every uproarious, wild little turn,
A lesson in joy, for all we discern.

Mirth in the Midst of Madness

The squirrel hoards crumbs, with flair and style,
While juggling acorns, it makes us smile.
A dog in a tutu, prancing with glee,
Dizzy from chasing its own shadowy spree.

When socks disappear, we raise an eyebrow,
The dryer's a thief; we hardly know how.
Shirts turn to kites, drifting in the breeze,
Crazy conclusions that truly tease.

Witty remarks in the oddest of times,
Elude the ordinary, flow like rhymes.
Chasing the punchlines like kids on the run,
In the book of absurd, we've hardly begun.

Yet, through the chaos, blooms pure delight,
As laughter erupts, banishing night.
With madness embraced, we caper and cheer,
For in that wild whirl, sense disappears.

Puns in the Narrative

A chicken crossed roads without any clue,
Quipping and quacking, making quite the view.
The fish told a joke, it's one for the books,
As it flopped on dry land, giving funny looks.

In the café, cups laugh, steam rising high,
Whispers of sugar, they wink as they fly.
The spoon and the fork, in skilful ballet,
Twist and retreat in a delightful display.

Words take wild turns, like a cat on a chase,
Chasing their tails in verbal embrace.
Puns melt like butter, smooth on the tongue,
In the narrative's dance, we're forever young.

So join this grand feast, where humor is spread,
In every good quip, a belly's well-fed.
Laughter's the garnish, we savor the fun,
As the tales keep spinning, long after we're done.

The Comic Canvas of Reality

A painter sips tea, spills color on dreams,
Drawing bright laughter in sun-kissed beams.
Every brushstroke's a giggle, a poke,
In the collage of whimsy, we riddle and joke.

The clock spins backward, time takes a break,
Puns flow like rivers, in playful awake.
Each tick-tock a chuckle, beneath the sun's gaze,
Crafting our moments in colorful haze.

Elbows are nudged in the gallery crowd,
Over spilled paint, outrageous and loud.
Fingers of fate dance in cosmic delight,
Creating the nonsense, the reason to write.

So let's stand together, in this vibrant frame,
Where laughter is canvas and joy is the aim.
With puns as our palette, we color the night,
In a world full of jest, everything feels right.

Comedy in Chaos

In the circus of days, we tumble and spin,
Juggling our troubles with a cheeky grin.
Clowns in our hearts, laughter on display,
Who knew absurdity would brighten the way?

With socks mismatched, we dance through the fray,
Blunders and bumbles, come join in the play.
Every slip-up, a punchline in disguise,
Turn frowns upside down, watch joy harmonize.

The world's a stage, or so it seems clear,
With acts full of blunders that tickle your ear.
Tickle your sides with a wink and a nod,
Embrace the chaos, for it's rather odd.

So let's raise a laugh with every small blight,
In the game of existence, we'll find our delight.
A jest in the madness, a grin in the rush,
Celebrate clumsy, let's dance in the hush.

Silliness of Truth

In the garden of nonsense, flowers bloom bright,
With petals of laughter that tickle the night.
Bees buzzing jokes as they flit to and fro,
While daisies gossip, "Do you think we can grow?"

The squirrels debate, beneath branches of green,
In a language of chuckles, quite silly, I mean.
The trees are conspiracy theorists at best,
Whispering tales of a homespun jest.

Each truth has a twist, like a pretzel's fine shape,
Folded and twisted, it's all quite a scrape.
With humor as seasoning to spice up the bland,
We'll dance through the quirks in this wonderful land.

So raise up your glass to the wisdom of jest,
In follies of fate, may we find our true quest.
For silliness reigns in the heart of it all,
Where laughter erupts, and the shadows will fall.

The Riddle of Existence

What's heavy and light, a puzzle of sorts,
A riddle and ruckus in oddball reports.
With questions like kites flying high in the blue,
Some answers are sticky, like gum on your shoe.

A duck in a bowtie speaks wisdom at dawn,
While cats read the cards in a game they've drawn.
The clock's lost its tick, yet it dances in time,
Searching for meaning in a nursery rhyme.

The sun wears a smile, as it peeks through the haze,
While shadows play tricks in a curious maze.
With every step taken, a giggle we find,
In the riddle of everything, joy interlined.

For existence, dear friend, is a jest wrapped in cheer,
A treasure trove of nonsense that draws us all near.
So ponder the quirks, the fun hidden deep,
In the mystery of living, may laughter not sleep.

Giggles in the Gloom

In twilight's embrace, when shadows are cast,
A chuckle erupts, and the frowns fade fast.
With giggles like fireflies, they flicker and shine,
Outshining the gloom, like a glass full of wine.

A penguin in slippers slips right by the door,
Waddling through worries, a wacky folklore.
Every mishap, a moment to cheer,
In the drapery of gloom, let's spread some good cheer.

The moon cackles softly, a jester on high,
Amid circling clouds, it plays with the sky.
For darkness, my friend, can be quite the delight,
When laughter finds refuge in the heart of the night.

So join in the chuckles, the joy amidst strife,
For each little giggle brings color to life.
In the shadowy corners where smiles seem to fade,
Let's twirl in the giggles that sorrow once made.

Capering Through the Unknown

In the circus of oddity, we prance,
Twirling in colors, giving fate a chance.
With each surprise, we leap and roll,
A tumble of moments, that's our goal.

Juggling our thoughts, we giggle and sway,
While the rhythm of chaos has its own way.
Tickling the strange, we share in the jest,
Finding our joy in the quirky quest.

So let the confusions come, we won't resist,
We'll dance through the riddles, too fun to miss.
With laughter our lantern, we'll stumble along,
In the absurdity, we've found our song.

Each twist in the tale, we take with a grin,
For it's the unpredictable where laughs begin.
When the world throws a punchline, we'll swing wide,
In the caper of life, we take it in stride.

Snickers of the Universe

Look up at the stars with a curious glance,
They twinkle and shimmer, a cosmic dance.
Giggles in silence, the planets conspire,
Witty little whispers, hearts catch fire.

Comets would roll their eyes, if they could,
At the quirks of existence, the misunderstood.
The moon winks slyly, with a twinkle of cheer,
As stardust chuckles, loud and clear.

In the vastness abounds, a hum of delight,
Where oddities flourish, and dreams take flight.
A canvas of wonder, painted in jest,
The universe chuckles, we're all guests.

So let's join the laughter, with stardust in hand,
In the snickers of cosmos, we take our stand.
Embrace the absurd, raise a glass to the night,
For the secrets of laughter make everything bright.

Eccentricities of Human Nature

With socks that don't match and hats on sideways,
We strut in our quirks, in comical ways.
In the zoo of our habits, we laugh and we play,
Each tickle of truth keeps the gloom at bay.

Whispers of folly fill every street,
With bursts of confusion, our lives are sweet.
A nod to the weird that we all can embrace,
In the laughter of moments, we find our place.

From the dance of the toddler to the sage's quip,
We sip on the wisdom that makes our hearts skip.
Each foible and fumble that adds to our tale,
Wraps us in laughter, like a soft, cozy veil.

So let's toast our flaws, the charm that they lend,
In the dance of the silly, we find a true friend.
For amidst all the mess, what's crucial to see,
Is that laughter's the thread that binds you and me.

The Peculiar Path to Insight

Through winding trails of confusion we trot,
With breadcrumbs of wisdom, connecting the dots.
We trip and we stumble, our maps upside down,
Yet laughter rings out, a jubilant sound.

In the maze of our minds, odd queries awake,
Each question a riddle, for curiosity's sake.
We pick up the pieces, patchwork our thoughts,
In the tangle of whims, there's treasure sought.

With every odd twist, we chuckle and learn,
For folly and insight have equal concern.
The road may be crooked, but joy takes the lead,
Planting seeds of humor, from which we proceed.

And when clarity strikes, it's rarely a chore,
In strange revelations, we revel and roar.
For the path that is peculiar, with laughter our guide,
Leads us to truth where joys collide.

When Seriousness Takes a Vacation

Caught in a whirlwind of giggles wide,
Silliness dances, my worries slide.
A puzzle unfolds, none can decipher,
The more we laugh, the less we suffer.

Ties loosen up; we twirl with glee,
Finding joy in absurdity's spree.
With every chuckle, a burden shed,
Reality giggles, and we follow ahead.

With seriousness gone, the norm can bend,
Every odd moment is a trendy friend.
Laughter rings out, echoing bright,
Chasing shadows away, igniting the night.

So here's to the farce, the slapstick spree,
A haven of fun, just you and me.
When smiles are scattered, nothing's amiss,
A vacation of humor, a jubilant bliss.

Laughing at the Cosmic Joke

Stars wink knowingly, a jest in the void,
We ponder the mysteries; galactic joy deployed.
With a cosmic chuckle, the universe sneers,
As we tumble through dreams, voiding our fears.

Planets spinning, a dance of the absurd,
In the stillness of space, we find every word.
The punchline's elusive, as chaos prevails,
Yet laughter persists in the grandest of tales.

Each quasar whispers secrets, we grin in return,
The humor of stardust in our hearts does burn.
Bright constellations guide our jovial way,
In the gallery of laughter, we dare to stay.

So let's toast to the heavens, a resounding cheer,
For it's the cosmic laughter that keeps us near.
With every twinkle, a jest we embrace,
In the grand hall of laughter, we find our place.

Comedic Reflections in the Mirror

Gazing in mirrors, with brows raised high,
A clownish grin meets a curious eye.
Whispers of mischief reflect back at me,
In this silly realm, we're forever free.

Shadows of humor dance on the wall,
Fleeting reflections that giggle and sprawl.
A smirk in the glass, eccentric delight,
Twists of the mind in the soft, golden light.

Tripping on thoughts that wobble and sway,
Funny faces emerge, leading the way.
Every shift brings a chuckle, pure glee,
In the world of reflections, we set ourselves free.

The mirror's a jester, a quirky old sage,
With wisdom in laughter, it's never beige.
Finding joy in flaws, so delightful and sweet,
A playful escape in this comical feat.

Ridiculous Roads Taken

Each path I wander is absurdly bright,
With signposts of nonsense, a delightful sight.
Bumping into laughter on every turn,
In the chaos of travels, fresh lessons I learn.

Traffic jams filled with jokes and jests,
Driving through madness, it's all in the tests.
Roads paved with laughter, cobbled with cheer,
Getting lost in the humor, that's the true steer.

GPS giggles at plans gone awry,
Finding new routes that make spirits fly.
With every misstep, we pave a new lane,
In the tapestry woven with joy and with pain.

So here's to the paths we so foolishly roam,
In the land of the quirky, we build our own home.
Each ridiculous road is a joyful surprise,
With friendship and laughter, we'll always rise.

The Haphazard Symphony

In the orchestra of chance we play,
Notes of laughter, echoes sway.
A conductor lost, a comic blunder,
Strikes of whimsy, rolling thunder.

When the violins twirl in clumsy dance,
And the drums trip over in a daze of chance.
A melody is born, absurd yet bright,
In this silly frolic, we find delight.

Trombones slide with a honking sound,
Winds blow breezy, joy is unbound.
With each sharp note, a giggle shared,
In this haphazard symphony, we dared.

So gather round, let us embrace,
The mess of sound, a playful space.
For in chaos, humor finds its home,
Together we laugh, forever we roam.

Joy's Playful Paradox

In rounds of giggles, and a twist or two,
The world spins funny, in a vibrant hue.
We ponder riddles beneath the sun,
In this whimsical dance, we all have fun.

Like cats in hats, and dogs on wheels,
The silliness of fate always appeals.
With each paradox, a grin unfolds,
Through the laughter, a truth that holds.

So tread on puddles and bounce on grass,
Taking joy in moments that swiftly pass.
In the curious mess, the magic is found,
As we puzzle upon humor, round and round.

For if we dare to turn our frown,
Every slip can lift us up from the ground.
In light-hearted jest, we embrace the ride,
Where joy and absurdity will always collide.

Unexpected Turns in the Comedy of Life

With a jump and a jive, we spin about,
In this comedy show, there's no doubt.
Each twist and turn, a surprise in store,
A punchline delivered, we howl for more.

Life walks in with mismatched shoes,
Playing tricks, spreading colorful hues.
With a wink and a chuckle, we play along,
For laughter, my friend, is what makes us strong.

Upside down and back again,
Chasing giggles, we're never plain.
In the circus of moments, we juggle delight,
Finding the joy in the flops and the flights.

So slip on the banana, take a tumble,
In this wild world, let's never grumble.
With unexpected turns, we dance and spin,
In the hilarious chaos, the fun begins.

Silliness as a Survival Tool

When the skies are gray, and the day feels tough,
A sprinkle of silly will be enough.
With jester hats and laughs that bloom,
We chase the shadows out of the room.

In moments of chaos, when woes ensue,
A wink and a nod can turn the view.
With giggles that bubble and tickle our soul,
We find in the folly our ultimate goal.

Like clowns on parade, we bounce and cheer,
Turning troubles into laughter, sincere.
With a side of absurd, we forge ahead,
In the realm of whimsy, our fears are shed.

So grab your joy, let it be your guide,
In the circus of life, let silliness ride.
For when all seems lost, remember this tool—
Laughter is magic, and it makes us cool.

When Logic Takes a Backseat

The chicken crossed the road, you see,
To chase a dream, wild and free.
But on the other side, it paused,
And asked the grass why it was so confused.

With socks on hands and shoes in trees,
It laughed and danced in the soft summer breeze.
For sometimes sense takes a holiday,
And leaves us giggling all the way.

A cat in a hat, with a curious grin,
Swayed to tunes, twirling in spin.
While dogs donned bows, sipping on tea,
The world turned silly, just let it be.

So relish the days when things go awry,
With witty quirks that flutter and fly.
Grab a chuckle, it's all in good jest,
When logic takes a nap, we're surely blessed.

Rambunctious Revelations

A fish in a suit, reading the news,
Spoke of the days wearing mismatched shoes.
The audience roared, from the trees to the ground,
In moments of madness, true wisdom is found.

A squirrel on a bicycle, racing the sun,
Determined to show it could truly run.
With acorns for brakes and leaves for a seat,
The laughter erupted, oh what a feat!

A penguin in pajamas, across the ice slid,
Claiming his tricycle came from a kid.
With all of the charm and none of the grace,
It's clear that absurdity reigns in this place.

In rambunctious times, join the frolicsome spree,
Find joy in the chaos, so wild and so free.
With each hearty chuckle, we summon the cheer,
For reveling in whimsy brings us all near.

Chuckles Wrapped in Lessons

A goat in a library, reading out loud,
Tales of the ocean, drawing a crowd.
With every bleat, a truth to be found,
In stories of woe, giggles abound.

The wise old owl in spectacles perched,
Taught us to laugh as the lessons were searched.
Between every quip, a moral came clear,
That folly can lead to wisdom sincere.

A frog on a lily, joined in the fun,
With jokes about flies chased under the sun.
The ripple of laughter broke echoes of doubt,
As nature revealed what life was about.

In moments of laughter, our spirits take flight,
With chuckles wrapped tightly, challenges light.
For in the midst of the goof and the jest,
We find truest teachings, we're truly blessed.

The Curious Case of Laughter

In a land made of candy, where rainbows reside,
A pickle donned glasses, took us for a ride.
It wobbled and jiggled, with no hint of care,
Everybody joined in with giggles to spare.

A snail with a rocket, zooming through space,
Declared with a grin that slow wins the race.
As planets chuckled and stars gave a wink,
We realized we'd never need to rethink.

A bear in a tutu danced under the moon,
Swirling in circles, humming a tune.
With fish as the backup, and crabs on the drum,
Together they created a whimsical hum.

So let's treasure the moments, absurd as they come,
For laughter transcends every tick and each thrum.
In the curious case where joy leads the way,
We find that together we're brighter each day.

www.ingramcontent.com/pod-product-compliance
Lightning Source LLC
Chambersburg PA
CBHW071834160426
43209CB00003B/292